Teaching

Contents

Sam Sorts it Out

The Mole who was Scared of the Dark

Batter Splatter!

The Samosa Thief

Something So Big

The House that Jack Built

Introduction

The *Snapdragons* series is a rich mix of different kinds of stories presented as picture books with expertly written text carefully levelled to provide reading practice at each stage in Key Stage 1.

This set of six books at Stage 6 provides further reading practice to encourage children to become competent readers. The first books in this stage have short, simple sentences, plenty of repetition and straightforward ideas, but as children work through the set they will find stories with a literary dimension and a more sophisticated tone and variety of language. These stories provide further practice in reading key words, as well as useful vocabulary, such as colour words, numbers, size and position, relating to the different contexts.

The books at Stage 6 include stories based in familiar settings that reflect everyday life, and the readers will quickly identify with the family members, school friends and pets and recognise their experiences. There are also animal fantasy tales and a new story based on a traditional nursery rhyme.

Children are encouraged to look at the illustrations for visual cues to the words in the text, and to find out what is happening in the story. The picture book presentation will also encourage children to tell the story in their own words so that they develop their oral skills.

How to introduce the books

Before reading the story for guided or independent reading, always read the title and talk about the picture on the cover.

Go through the book together, looking at the pictures and talking about them. If there are context words (listed in the chart on page 4) that are new or unfamiliar, point them out and read them with the children. Read the story to the children, encouraging confident children to join in with you.

This booklet provides prompts and suggestions for using the books in groups and for guided, group and independent activities, matched to text, sentence and word level objectives. There are also separate Guided Reading Cards available for six titles at each stage. Suggestions are also provided for speaking and listening activities, writing activities, and cross-curricular links. You can use these suggestions to follow on from your reading or at another time.

Reading notes are also provided in each book. They can be found on the inside front and back covers of each book. These suggest friendly prompts and activities for parents or carers reading with their children at home.

Reading skills

Stage 6 develops:

- strategies for independent reading, including consolidation of irregular phonological and spelling patterns
- insights into feelings and motivation of characters
- a wider sight vocabulary
- awareness of other viewpoints
- confidence through familiarity with the characters and the format
- sustained independent writing.

Vocabulary chart

Stage 6		
Sam Sorts it Out	Year 2 High frequency words	can't could do door down first for good had her his house just last made next not now old out over ran so some that then time too took tree us very were what when would your
	Context words	paddling pool waterfall spanner screwdriver bucket hose banana monster spade hammer
The Mole who was Scared of the Dark	Year 2 High frequency words	about again another as be but by could did do don't down got had have help him his how if just little lived love made next night not off one out over ran so that there time too took two very were what when with your black pink
	Context words	mole dark tunnel scared wriggly tickly worm monster centipede
Batter Splatter!	Year 2 High frequency words	an another back be called came do don't door down first from good have her his jump(ed) just make more must now one our out over ran school some that them then three time two us very want way were what when will with
	Context words	pancake eggs flour milk visitor batter ceiling headache
The Samosa Thief	Year 2 High frequency words	after an back brother but came can't could did down got had have his how if jump(ed) made make more new not now one out over put ran saw so some their them then too took us very were what when who will with
	Context words	samosa kitchen shelf thief video recorder
Something So Big	Year 2 High frequency words	about back be because but by came don't down from good got had have help here his little lived much not off one our over put seen so that them then there too us water way what when where will with
	Context words	Creepies Crawlies flowers leaf alone tickle hero
The House that Jack Built	Year 2 High frequency words	back be but door first had here his home house just live made make more much new now out so that these there were where who with would
	Context words	spade square concrete bricks tiles glass nails paint

Curriculum coverage chart

Stage 6	Speaking and listening	Reading	Writing
Sam Sorts it Out			
NLS/SLL	Y2T1 15, 16	T3, S2, W7	T11
Scotland	Level A/B	Level A/B	Level A/B
N. Ireland	Activities: a, b, c, g Outcomes: a, b, c, d	Activities: a, b, c, e Outcomes: b, c, d, e, f, g	Outcomes: a, b, c, e, h, i
Wales	Range: 1, 3, 5 Skills: 1, 2, 3, 4	Range: 1, 2, 4, 5, 6 Skills: 1, 2, 4	Range: 1, 2, 3, 7 Skills: 1, 3, 4, 5, 7, 8
The Mole who was Scared of the Dark			
NLS/SLL	S3/Y2T1 13	T5, S2, W1	T11
Scotland	Level A/B	Level A/B	Level A/B
N. Ireland	Activities: a, b Outcomes: b, c, d, f, g	Activities: a, b Outcomes: b, c, d, f, k	Outcomes: b, c, e, h, i
Wales	Range: 1, 5 Skills: 1, 2	Range: 1, 2, 4, 5, 6 Skills: 1, 2, 4	Range: 1, 2, 3, 7 Skills: 1, 3, 7, 8
Batter Splatter!			
NLS/SLL	Y2T1 16	T4, S3, W2	T15
Scotland	Level A/B	Level A/B	Level A/B
N. Ireland	Activities: a, b, c, e Outcomes: a, d, c, d	Activities: a, b Outcomes: b, c, d, f	Outcomes: b, c, e, h, i
Wales	Range: 1, 5 Skills: 1, 2, 3	Range: 1, 2, 4, 5, 6 Skills: 1, 2, 4	Range: 1, 2, 3, 4, 7 Skills: 1, 3, 5, 7, 8
The Samosa Thief			
NLS/SLL	Y2T1 16	T3, S6, W8	T10
Scotland	Level A/B	Level A/B	Level A/B
N. Ireland	Activities: a, b, c, f Outcomes: a, b, c, d	Activities: a, b, c, e, f Outcomes: b, c, d, e, f, g	Outcomes: a, b, c
Wales	Range: 1, 5 Skills: 1, 2, 3, 4	Range: 1, 2, 4, 5, 6 Skills: 1, 2, 4	Range: 1, 2, 3, 7 Skills: 1, 3, 5, 7, 8
Something So Big			
NLS/SLL	Y2T1 13	T5, S5, W4	S6
Scotland	Level A/B	Level A/B	Level A/B
N. Ireland	Activities: a, b, h Outcomes: b, c, d, f	Activities: a, b, c Outcomes: b, c, d, f, k	Outcomes: b, h, i
Wales	Range: 1, 2 Skills: 1, 2	Range: 1, 2, 4, 5, 6 Skills: 1, 2, 4	Range: 3, 4 Skills: 2, 6, 8
The House that Jack Built			
NLS/SLL	Y2T1 13	T7, S1, W8	T12
Scotland	Level A/B	Level A/B	Level A/B
N. Ireland	Activities: a, b, c, h Outcomes: d, f, g	Activities: a, b, c, e Outcomes: b, c, d, f, j, k	Outcomes: a, b, c, h, i
Wales	Range: 5 Skills: 1, 2	Range: 1, 2, 4, 5, 6 Skills: 1, 2, 4	Range: 2, 3, 4, 7 Skills: 1, 3, 7, 8

Sam Sorts it Out

Reading the story

Introducing the story

- Look together at the front cover, read the title and the author's name.
- Ask the children to look briefly through the book and point out that it contains two stories. Ask them to read the titles of the two stories.
- Ask the children to suggest what the stories will be about, and find the names of the main characters.

During reading

- Prompt the children to use different strategies in order to work out new or difficult words (checking the illustrations for cues, breaking words into smaller chunks, e.g. p3 "padd/ling", "wat/er/fall", p4 "screw/driv/er").
- Praise the children when they self-correct without prompting.
- Praise children when they read using an expressive tone, taking note of question marks and exclamation marks.

Observing Check that the children:
- take account of the punctuation to read with expression
- understand how the title of the book "Sam Sorts it Out" links the two story themes.

Group and independent reading activities

Text level work

Range familiar setting/predictable and patterned language

Objective To be aware of the difference between spoken and written language through comparing oral recounts with text; make use of formal story elements in re-telling (T3).

You will need six word cards of connectives that are used to link sentences and paragraphs: Then, Next, At first, At last, When, Later.

- Ask the children to work with a partner and share a set of word cards.

- Ask them to take turns to re-tell the stories to each other, choosing different connectives to link parts of their re-tellings.
- Ask them to compare their re-tellings with the text by finding the connectives and noting how or when the author used them in the stories.

Observing Do the children choose connectives to help them sequence the events in the stories?

Sentence level work

Objective To find examples, in fiction and non-fiction, of words and phrases that link sentences (S2).

- Ask the children to look through the stories and find all the words that are used to link sentences and show the sequence of events.
- Ask them to add the words to their personal word banks.

Observing Do the children read the text carefully on each page? Do they find other linking words that were not included in the Text-level activity, e.g. "But", "And", "Afterwards"?

Word level work

Objective To use word endings, e.g. "ed" (past tense), "ing" (present tense) to support their reading and spelling (W7).

- Write the word "play" on the board, and model how to change the verb into past tense and present tense by adding the appropriate endings. Write them on the board as column headings, e.g.

  play   played   playing
- Ask the children to look through the text and find other verbs that can have "ed" and "ing" endings. Ask them to write them in columns under the headings.

Observing Do the children identify any irregular verbs that do not have "ed" as a past tense ending, e.g. p15 "took", p18 "dug"? Do children find any words where the consonant is doubled before the endings are added, e.g. p9 "tipped" (tip, tipping), p24 "ran" (running)?

Speaking and listening activities

Objectives To listen to each other's views and preferences, agree next steps to take and identify contributions by each group member (Y2T1 15); To adopt appropriate roles in small or large groups and consider alternative courses of action (Y2T1 16).

- Discuss Sam's character with the children, how he "sorts it out" and likes to find solutions to problems.
- Ask the children to suggest some new problems for Sam to solve, e.g. how to stop birds eating plants in the vegetable garden, how to stop the rain making their sand pit wet.
- Ask the children to work in small groups of two or three, and to talk about how Sam would solve the problem, and then to act it out.

Cross-curricular link
◀▶ PSHE: take part in discussions with one other person and the whole class

Writing

Objective To use language of time (see Sentence level work) to structure a sequence of events (T11).

- Discuss new problems for Sam to solve (see Speaking and listening activity).
- Model writing a new short story about Sam based on the children's suggestions, and discuss which connectives to use to link the events.
- Ask the children to write their own story in which Sam sorts it out.

The Mole who was Scared of the Dark

Reading the story

Introducing the story

- Look together at the cover. Read the title and author's name.
- Discuss the cover illustration with the children. Ask: *How do you think the little mole feels?*
- Ask the children to find the word "Scared" on the cover.
- Look briefly through the pages and identify any vocabulary that may prove difficult, e.g. p6 "wriggly", p9 "centipede".

During reading

- Praise the children when they follow the text with their eyes and self-correct as they read.
- Prompt the children to use the pictures and initial sounds to help them read the interest words.
- Praise children when they read words previously identified with confidence, e.g. "scared", "wriggly", "centipede".
- Encourage the children to segment difficult words to help work them out, e.g. p3 "diff/er/ent", p7 "tick/ly", p8 "mon/ster", p21 "dis/co/very".

Observing Check that the children:
- use a mixture of strategies to work out difficult words
- make use of the punctuation to help them read with an expressive tone.

Group and independent reading activities

Text level work

Range fantasy world/predictable and patterned language

Objective To identify and discuss reasons for events in stories, linked to plot (T5).

- Ask the children: *Why was Little Mole scared of the dark? Find a page that gives a reason.* (pages 6, 7, 8 and 9)
- Ask the children: *Why was Little Mole feeling sad and left out? Find a page that gives a reason.* (pages 14 and 15)

● Ask: *What did Dad Mole do to help Little Mole? Find a page that gives the answer.* (page 17)

Observing Are the children able to support their answers with evidence from the text?

Sentence level work

Objective To find examples, in fiction and non-fiction, of words and phrases that link sentences (S2).

● Ask the children to read page 8 and find a phrase that shows the passage of time. ("The next day")
● Ask the children to suggest other words or phrases that show time passing in stories, e.g. later, next, after a while, then, soon. Draw up a list of their suggestions on the board.
● Ask the children to work with a partner and take turns (taking alternate pages) to re-tell the story to each other, using the illustrations as a prompt. Ask them to use some of the words from the list on the board to link the episodes.

Observing Do the children choose sensible connectives to link their re-tellings? Do they recall the sequence of events?

Word level work

Objective To secure identification, spelling and reading of long vowel digraphs in simple words from Y1 term 3 (W1).

● Write the word "down" and "about" on the board.
● Emphasise the "ow" sound in both words. Ask the children to look carefully through the text and identify any other words with the same sound. ("shouting", "out", "shouted", "proud")
● Ask the children to write the words they found on their whiteboards, and to say if the sound is spelt "ou" or "ow".
● Encourage the children to suggest other words from their own knowledge that have the same sound, but have the "ow" spelling pattern, e.g. crown, frown, clown.
● Ask the children to write the words on their boards as a separate list, and practise spelling them using Look, Cover, Write and Check.

Observing Do the children recognise the same spelling but different sound in "down" and "own" on page 17?

Speaking and listening activities

Objectives To recognise and take account of commas and exclamation marks in reading aloud with appropriate expression (S3); To speak with clarity and use intonation when reading and reciting texts (Y2T1 13).

- Divide the class into two groups and ask the children to read the story aloud, each group taking alternate pages.
- Encourage the children to use expressive voices, particularly when reading the dialogue, by taking account of question marks and exclamation marks.

Cross-curricular link
◄► Science: animals that have their homes underground

Writing

Objective To use language of time to structure a sequence of events (T11).

- Discuss the story plot with the children and ask them to say as briefly as they can what happens.
- Remind the children of the list of "time" vocabulary from the Sentence Level activity.
- Ask the children to write a précis of the story using the "time" vocabulary to link their sentences.
- Suggest they use no more than fifty words to ensure they keep their précis short.

Batter Splatter!

Reading the story

Introducing the story

- Look at the front cover and read the title. Discuss the illustration with the children and ask them to suggest what the story might be about.
- Look through the pages, talking about what happens in the illustrations.
- Identify any new or difficult words in the text, e.g. p6 "stirring", p12 "ceiling".
- Look at the pages where "SPLAT" is written. Ask the children why it is written in this way, and how they should read it in the story.

During reading

- Praise the children when they read with fluency.
- If children misread a word, suggest they reread the whole sentence or passage to correct the mistake.
- Encourage the children to read with expression, particularly taking account of exclamation marks in dialogue.
- As the children read, occasionally ask them to describe what is happening in the illustrations to ensure they are following the story.

Observing Check that the children:
- self-correct, using a range of strategies
- read "SPLAT" with appropriate expression, and take note of punctuation.

Group and independent reading activities

Text level work

Range familiar setting/predictable and patterned language

Objective To understand time and sequential relationships in stories, i.e. what happened when (T4).

You will need the following parts of sentences written on strips of paper, or written randomly on the board:

It was Pancake Day so...
the children made pancakes.
A visitor was coming to school so...

the children wanted to make their best pancakes.
Asha tossed a pancake but...
it landed in the bin.
Harry tossed a pancake but...
it stuck on the ceiling.
The visitor came to the classroom and...
a pancake fell on her hat.

- Give the children the mixed-up parts of sentences and ask them to put them into a sequence to retell the story.
- Ask the children to use their sequence to retell the story to a partner.

Observing Do the children understand that each event has a cause?

Sentence level work

Objective To recognise and take account of commas and exclamation marks in reading aloud with appropriate expression (S3).

- Ask the children to work with a partner.
- Ask them to reread the story by taking turns to read the dialogue only.
- Ask some pairs of children to read the dialogue aloud to the class, with the other children following the text in the book.

Observing Do the children use expressive voices appropriate to the punctuation?

Word level work

Objective To revise and extend the reading and spelling of words containing different spellings of the long vowel phonemes from Year 1 (W2).

- Tell the children they are going to be word detectives and find all the words with the long vowel sound "ee" in the text.
- Ask the children to tell you some of the words they have found. Write them on the board, so that the different spelling patterns provide headings for a list, e.g. "need", "here", "ceiling", "each".
- Ask them to write their words in lists according to their spelling patterns.
- Ask them to add other words, from their own experience, to their lists.

Do the children understand that some vowel sounds have different spellings?

Speaking and listening activities

Objective To adopt appropriate roles in small or large groups and consider alternative courses of action (Y2T1 16).

- Ask the children to take turns to sit in the hot seat and take the role of the "important visitor".
- Ask the children in the hot seat to describe their visit to the school and add a further episode when they left the school, e.g. when the visitor got home and found the pancake.

Cross-curricular link
◀▶ PSHE: taking care when cooking

Writing

Objective To write simple instructions (T15).

- Discuss what the children in the story did to make their pancakes.
- Draw up a list of ingredients on the board, and discuss the steps needed to be taken, and the order they should be in.
- Model how to write one or two of the steps.
- Ask the children to write the rest of the instructions as a simple recipe for a cookery book.

The Samosa Thief

Reading the story

Introducing the story

- Look at the front cover and read the title. Ask the children to find the word "Thief" in the title.
- Ask the children if they like samosas, and ask them to suggest who might steal some.
- Look at pages 2 and 3 together. Read the text and together identify the characters in the illustration.
- Ask the children to continue reading independently.

During reading

- Praise the children when they follow the text with their eyes, only finger-pointing when they have difficulty.
- If children have difficulty with any vocabulary, encourage them to check the illustration, reread and suggest a word that makes sense.
- On page 11, ask the children to read Mum's direct speech with appropriate expression.
- At the end of the story, ask the children if they had guessed who the thief was.

Observing Check that the children:
- ■ read the high frequency words on sight
- ■ recognise speech marks to denote direct speech
- ■ use a range of strategies to work out difficult words.

Group and independent reading activities

Text level work

Range familiar setting/predictable and patterned language

Objective To be aware of the difference between spoken and written language through comparing oral recounts with text; make use of formal story elements in retelling (T3).

- Ask the children to work with a partner.
- Ask them to take turns to describe the story to each other.
- Ask them to return to the text, and identify anything that was different in their descriptions.

- Encourage the children to use appropriate vocabulary to say how their descriptions vary from the written text, e.g. direct speech, connectives.

Observing Are the children able to recall the story without referring to the book?

Sentence level work

Objective To use a variety of simple organisational devices, e.g. arrows, lines, boxes, keys, to indicate sequences and relationships (S6).

- Ask the children to turn to pages 2 and 3.
- Ask them to find the names of the characters in the text and match them to the illustrations.
- Ask them to draw a picture representing each character, write the character's name, and their relationship to each other linked by lines or arrows, e.g. Sunita – sister to – Sanjay – brother to – Raj – brother to – Sunita, and so on.

Observing Are the children able to identify each character from the story and understand their family relationships?

Word level work

Objective To secure understanding and use of the terms "vowel" and "consonant" (W8).

- Write the terms "vowel" and "consonant" on the board.
- Ask the children to write the names of each character, and then to list the vowels and consonants in their names under the correct heading.
- Ask them to then work with a partner, and challenge each other to find words with only one, then two, then three vowels, or consonants, on different pages.

Observing Are the children confident about which letters are vowels and consonants? Do the children find the words quickly and easily, scanning the lines of text?

Speaking and listening activities

Objective To adopt appropriate roles in small or large groups and consider alternative courses of action (Y2T1 16).

- Discuss what else Sunita and Sanjay could have done to find out who the thief was, e.g. hiding and watching.
- Provide the children with stick-puppets of the characters of Benji, Sunita and Sanjay and ask groups to act out the story with a new plan to identify the thief.

Cross-curricular link
◄► PSHE: belonging to various groups and communities, e.g. families

Writing

Objective To use story structure to write about own experience in same/similar form (T10).

- Discuss the children's favourite food that they eat in their own homes.
- Draw up a list from their suggestions. Ask them to say why they like it best, and what they do or think when it is cooking.
- Model writing a short paragraph about one of the foods for the children to use as a model and adapt, e.g.
    My favourite food is…
    When My Mum/Dad cooks it I always…

Something So Big
Reading the story

Introducing the story
- Look at the front cover and read the title. Ask the children what they think "Something So Big" might be.
- Look together at the illustration on pages 2 and 3, and discuss where the story is set. Ask the children to find the insect that was pictured on the front cover.
- Ask the children to look through the rest of the illustrations in the book to confirm the setting.

During reading
- Prompt the children to use the illustrations to help them work out words when they have difficulty.
- Ask the children to identify words that begin with capital letters inside sentences, and remind them that names begin with capital letters.
- On pages 8 and 9, ask the children to follow the words "Tum-tiddy-tum…" with a finger to show Bill Hooley's journey, and to read the words as if he was humming to himself.
- On page16, ask the children to read the words in italic print with expression.
- On page 19, ask the children to read the last word "A-W-A-K-E" as if this is scary for Bill Hooley.

Observing   Check that the children:
- recognise the different uses of print in the text and use them to read with appropriate expression
- read with fluency, only slowing when they meet new or difficult vocabulary.

Group and independent reading activities

Text level work
Range   fantasy world/predictable and patterned language

Objective   To identify and discuss reasons for events in stories, linked to plot (T5).

- Ask the children to suggest which word we use when we want to find out a reason for something. (why)
- Ask them to work with a partner, and to look through the text, taking alternate pages and asking each other a "why" question about what Bill Hooley does in the story.

Observing Do the children find the reasons for the events in the story, and use "because" in their answers?

Sentence level work

Objective To revise knowledge about other uses of capitalisation, e.g. for names, headings, titles, emphasis and begin to use in own writing (S5).

- Ask the children to look through the text and find the names of the characters in the story.
- Ask the children to explain how they know they are characters' names. (capitalisation and the sense of a sentence)
- Ask the children to look through the text and find other ways the author has used capital letters and to suggest reasons why.

Observing Do the children differentiate between capital letters used for the beginning of a sentence and for other purposes?

Word level work

Objective To investigate and classify words with the same sounds but different spellings (W4).

- Read the names of Bill Hooley's friends on page 2, and emphasise the "or" sound in "Crawlies". Write the word on the board.
- Ask the children to find another word on the pages with the same sound ("watering" or "watered"). Add the word to the board.
- Ask the children to scan the text to find any other words with the same vowel sound and to write them on their boards.
- Ask the children to look at page 21, and suggest a verb to describe what Something So Big does with the water. If they cannot think of "pour" suggest it to them.
- Add "pour" to the list, and ask the children to add any other "or" words they can think of, and to group according to their spelling patterns.

Speaking and listening activities

Objective To speak with clarity and use intonation when reading and reciting texts (Y2T1 13).

- Ask the children to work with a partner and read alternate pages aloud to each other.
- Encourage the children to make full use of punctuation and font effects so that they read with an expression appropriate to the story.

Cross-curricular link

◀▶ Science: plants and animals in the local environment

Writing

Objective To use a variety of simple organisational devices, e.g. arrows, lines, boxes, keys, to indicate sequences and relationships (S6).

- Discuss the setting of the story with the children, and look through the text to work out Bill Hooley's journey.
- Model how to draw a story map to show the start of the journey.
- Ask the children to draw their own story map to show where the journey began and ended, and add other places in between. Ask them to write labels to describe each point on the journey.

The House that Jack Built

Reading the story

Introducing the story

- Look at the front cover and read the title. Ask the children if the title is familiar to them.
- Look at the illustration on the cover, and ask the children if they think this story will be the same as the familiar "The House that Jack Built"?
- Ask the children to look through the book at the illustrations to confirm their ideas. Ask them to say how this story differs from the traditional rhyme.

During reading

- Encourage the children to look for rhyming words, e.g. p2 "a lad who had", p4 "the plan that first began", and to read the text rhythmically where there are rhymes within sentences.
- Prompt the children to reread, to predict, and to use the illustrations to help them work out words when they have difficulty.
- Encourage the children to read the words that show actions and sounds in an expressive voice.
- On page 24, encourage the children to increase in speed as they read the noises.

Observing Check that the children:
- recognise rhyming words and sounds within words, e.g. p12 "pile"/"shiny"/"tiles"
- read with fluency, only slowing when they meet new or difficult vocabulary.

Group and independent reading activities

Text level work

Range familiar setting/new spin on a traditional nursery rhyme

Objective To learn, reread and recite favourite poems, taking account of punctuation; to comment on aspects such as word combinations, sound patterns (such as rhymes, rhythms, alliterative patterns) and forms of presentation (T7).

- Ask the children to work with a partner, and to take turns to read alternate pages, ignoring the action/sound words in the illustrations.
- Ask the children to look through the text and collect examples of rhyming words in these lines of text.
- Ask the children to say how the rhymes affect their reading.

Observing Do the children read their lines clearly and fluently?

Sentence level work

Objective To use awareness of grammar to decipher new or unfamiliar words, e.g. to predict from the text; to read on, leave a gap and reread (S1).

You will need the following sentences from the story with missing words:

> This is Jack, a lad who had no _____ to live.
> Here is the plan that first _____ the house that Jack built.
> I'll build my house here in this nice quiet _____.
> He dug a big _____, just where the house would be.
> It made a strong _____ to hold up the walls.
> They _____ the walls of the house that Jack built.

Also provide a list of words to fill in the spaces from the text:
  place   began   square   floor   coloured
and 12 alternative words, including the following:
  where   started   spot   rectangle   base   coloured

- Ask the children to find the sentences in the text and the missing word, and then to choose an alternative word from the list, making sure the sentences still make sense.

Observing Do the children choose new words with similar meanings to keep the sense of the sentences?

Word level work

Objective To secure understanding of the terms "vowel" and "consonant" (W8).

- Remind the children about which letters of the alphabet are vowels.
- Look together at page 2 of the text and identify words with one, two, and three vowels. (e.g. one: "is"; two: "place"; three: "house")

- Ask the children to search through the rest of the text and find words with three, four and five vowels. (three: "house", "concrete", "quiet", "square", "inside", "finished", "meeow", "peace", "noise"; four: "coloured"; five: "beautiful")

Observing   Do the children scan the text, and look for words by length?

Speaking and listening activities

Objective   To speak with clarity and use intonation when reading and reciting texts (Y2T1 13).

- Divide the class into two groups.
- Ask one group to read the lines of text that tell the story, and the other group to read the action/sound words, and to do actions to match them.

Cross-curricular link
◀▶ PHSE: play and work co-operatively

Writing

Objective   To use simple poetry structures and to substitute own ideas, write new lines (T12).

- Point out how lots of the pages in the book end with the words "the house that Jack built".
- Explain to the children that they are going to write their own versions of the story.
- Discuss other things that Jack could make, e.g. a car, a sandcastle, a cake.
- Model how to write some lines using the same text pattern as the book's, e.g.
  > This is the recipe that began the cake that Jack baked.
  > This is the flour that went in the cake that Jack baked.
  > This is the jam that went inside the cake that Jack baked.
- Ask the children to continue the pattern.

Oxford Reading Tree resources at this level

There is a range of material available at a similar level to these stories which can be used for consolidation or extension.

Stage 6

Teacher support
- Teacher's Handbook
- Take-Home Card for each story
- Storytapes
- Woodpeckers Photocopy Masters
- Group Activity Sheets Book 3 Stages 6–9
- ORT Games Stages 6–9

Further reading
- Oxford Reading Tree Storybooks for Core Reading
- Woodpeckers Phonics Anthologies 2–5
- Playscripts Stages 6 & 7
- Fireflies Non-Fiction
- Fact Finders Units D and E
- Glow-worms Poetry

Electronic
- Clip Art
- Stage 6 & 7 Talking Stories
- ORT Online www.OxfordReadingTree.com
- Floppy and Friends

OXFORD
UNIVERSITY PRESS

Great Clarendon Street, Oxford OX2 6DP

Oxford University Press is a department of the University of Oxford. It furthers the University's objective of excellence in research, scholarship, and education by publishing worldwide in

Oxford New York

Auckland Cape Town Dar es Salaam Hong Kong Karachi
Kuala Lumpur Madrid Melbourne Mexico City Nairobi
New Delhi Shanghai Taipei Toronto

With offices in

Argentina Austria Brazil Chile Czech Republic France Greece
Guatemala Hungary Italy Japan Poland Portugal Singapore
South Korea Switzerland Thailand Turkey Ukraine Vietnam

Oxford is a registered trade mark of Oxford University Press
in the UK and in certain other countries

© Oxford University Press 2005

The moral rights of the author have been asserted

Database right Oxford University Press (maker)

First published 2005

British Library Cataloguing in Publication Data

Data available

Series advisor Shirley Bickler

Cover illustrations by Charlotte Canty

Teacher's Notes: ISBN 0 19 8455860

10 9 8 7 6 5 4 3 2

Page make-up by Fakenham Photosetting, Fakenham, Norfolk

Printed in Great Britain by Ashford Colour Press, Gosport, Hants